WISDOM
FOR
CHILDREN

Princess Dumebi Grace

AuthorHouse™
1663 Liberty Drive
Bloomington, IN 47403
www.authorhouse.com
Phone: 1 (800) 839-8640

Scripture quotations marked KJV are from the Holy Bible, King James Version (Authorized Version). First published
in 1611. Quoted from the KJV Classic Reference Bible, Copyright © 1983 by The Zondervan Corporation.

Published by AuthorHouse 07/22/2015

ISBN: 978-1-5049-2211-1 (sc)
ISBN: 978-1-5049-2232-6 (e)

Print information available on the last page.

Any people depicted in stock imagery provided by Thinkstock are models,
and such images are being used for illustrative purposes only.
Certain stock imagery © Thinkstock.

This book is printed on acid-free paper.

Because of the dynamic nature of the Internet, any web addresses or links contained in this book may have changed
since publication and may no longer be valid. The views expressed in this work are solely those of the author and do not
necessarily reflect the views of the publisher, and the publisher hereby disclaims any responsibility for them.

authorHOUSE®

The Perfect Little Gift

To

From

ON THE OCCASION OF
(WRITE A PERSONAL MESSAGE)

Children are the heritage of the Lord as it is written in the bible, which means children are primarily from The Source, that is God. We may not have realized up until this point in our evolution that children make choices too just as adults do. Making a decision or choice is as difficult or easy for a child as it is for an adult. Knowing this fact will help parents train children differently and also encourage children to make decisions and actions in wisdom. Wisdom is therefore the principal thing to be taught and to learn for a child.

The wisdom you learn will help you live right on this planet earth so you don't get lost. The first lesson of wisdom every child should know on this plain to avoid confusion, is to recognize THE SOURCE. Where we come from and the powers we have to create our reality as we are co-creators with source energy.

Another lesson to learn is the wisdom of expression, how to communicate with others on this plain, how to understand others as well as being understood. How to express emotions of different type, how to guard our thoughts because out of it are the out issues of life. How to find and identify our purpose on this earth. Wisdom will guide you, if you find it. How do you then find or seek out wisdom. To get wisdom, you must ask the Source (God) to show you and teach you. When you ask, then God will tell you directly or show you books and materials to learn from to gain knowledge, when you practice the knowledge you have learnt, that is wisdom. Wisdom is know - how. Infinite mind could also bring people around you to learn from them, sometimes, it's from their mistakes or your own mistakes so you don't repeat them. Wisdom will make you understand that age doesn't make you wise but your willingness and desire to live with wisdom. Once you find wisdom, you have found, wealth, beauty, honour, praises, peace, excellent expression, fame if that's what you want, excellent relationships, love, the best education, gratitude, a happy fulfilled and an amazing life.

Find wisdom, get wisdom, live wise, live free, God speed!

Acknowledgments

All thanks and glory to the Divine Mind, the I AM and everyone who has encouraged me and taught me lessons on this plain called earth. I thank my family, especially my dad, my big brother Anthony, aunty Doris, my sister Lydia and her husband Mudi Akpocha for holding things down for me when I needed them most. I thank my biggest supporter, King Duru, who tells me I can always do better. I thank my friends, Uche Ken, Bash Elliott, April Quiana, Molly, for being there for me. I appreciate you all. My baby, Celynez, for your patience and understanding with mummy. My maternal uncle Prince Jude Nwoko for your care and support out here in the USA. My salute goes to my big cousin, HRH Charles Anyasi, the King of Idumujeunor Kingdom, for your support, brotherly advice and words of wisdom. I remember all what you say to me. Thanks to my laywer, Barr Victor Ogoli for taking care of things for me. My sincere appreciation goes to Erin Cohen, my publishing consultant and the Authorhouse team for making this project comes alive in all its beauty and splendor. You guys rock!

Thank you all for your prayers and good energy thoughts towards me. I feel it. I send loving energy back to y'all. I pray your wishes be fulfilled.

THANK YOU!!

DEDICATED TO

Celynez..I love you.

Other mini books in the series

- Wisdom for Riches

- Wicked Wisdom

- Wisdom Calls Again

- What is Wisdom for Women

My son, fear thou the LORD and the

king:

and meddle not with

them that are given to change:

Pro 24:21

Be respectful of people in authority. Don't
be friends with mediocre and people
that do not have plans
for their lives

Affirmations: I am noble and conscientious, I
understand the place of power and leadership.

I respect authority. I am wise.

My son, hear the instruction of thy father, and forsake not the law of thy mother:

Pro 1:8

You will be a source of joy to
your parents and family.

Affirmations: I am in this world to bring
happiness first to my parents, siblings, my
Immediate family and the rest of the world.

Thy father and thy

mother shall be glad, and she that bare thee

shall rejoice.

Pro 23:25

An African tale tells about a wise child who doesn't have a mother but listens in secret to the advice of another woman to her children and becomes great.

If you have parents who correct you and teach you by instructions, be wise to obey as there are other children who wish they had parents.

Listen to instructions and save yourself from the many troubles of life.

Affirmations: I am wise enough to take instructions

Never consider doing wrong.
You should never change to be
bad because of the world or
what you can get.
Affirmations: I am determined and I choose to
be good always.

The father of the
righteous shall greatly
rejoice: and he that
begetteth a wise child shall have joy of him.

Pro 23:24

A child that does good

is a righteous child and a

righteous child is wise.

Your family will be

proud of you.

Affirmations: I am thankful I do right and make

everyone around me and myself proud and thankful.

My son, if sinners entice thee, consent

thou not.

Pro 1:10

For the merchandise of it is
better than the
merchandise of silver, and the
gain thereof than fine gold.

Pro 3:14

The mere fact that your parents have

grown old and may not

understand latest trends

and technologies,

doesn't give you the right

to disrespect them in any way.

Affirmations: my parents are smart and always

wise. I love my parents and family.

*Hearken unto thy
father that begat thee,
and despise not thy
mother when
she is old.*

Pro 23:22

To have wisdom is to know how to apply
knowledge and it is better than riches
and wealth. There is wisdom for different things
There is a wisdom to make wealth, wisdom is still better than
wealth because you will always be able to make wealth.

Affirmations: I choose to be wise. (repeat)

Wisdom will help you live long
and fulfilled.

Affirmations: I am living a happy and fulfilled
life daily because I chose to be wise.

*My son, if thine heart
be wise, my heart shall rejoice, even
mine.*

Pro 23:15

A smart child makes

happy parents.

Affirmations: I am happy and I am grateful, my

family is happy because of me.

Hear, O my son, and

receive my sayings; and

the years of thy life shall

be many.

Pro 4:10

And why wilt thou, my son, be ravished

with a strange woman, and embrace the

bosom of a stranger?

Pro 5:20

Affirmations: I grow in wisdom,
knowledge and understanding daily, I am not
deceived, I am brilliant and focused
to achieve my life's purpose of love,
happiness and wealth with ease. I carry the presence of God.

Train up a child in the way he should

go: and when he is old, he will not

depart from it.

Pro 22:6

Do not have casual sex also known as a

fling or

patronize prostitutes

Affirmations: I choose to stay away from all

sexual temptations until I find my life partner

(soul mate) and we are married.

To be a simple person is
unwise, search out wisdom and
you will get understanding.
Affirmations: I am young but I am grateful to be
wise and I make informed decisions because I
have understanding.

The blueness of a
wound cleanseth
away evil: so do
stripes the inward parts of the belly.

Pro 20:30

Punishment will not kill you,

It will only make you a better person, leading

you to perfection.

Affirmations: I am perfect, corrective measures

by parents and loved ones will guide me to

success with Gods wisdom.

And beheld among the simple ones, I

discerned among the youths, a

young man void of understanding,

Pro 7:7

The proverbs of Solomon. A wise son

maketh a glad father: but a foolish son

is the heaviness of his mother.

Pro 10:1

Use your physical and mental strength
well while you are still young.
Affirmations: I am young, I am power and
strength, I am upbeat and determined. I am
grateful for my youthfulness and health.

The glory of young men
is their strength: and the beauty of
old men is the
gray head.

Pro 20:29

Look into the eyes of your
parents and siblings and you
will understand how sad your folly
makes them.

They expect more from you.
Affirmations: I am a blessing to myself, my
family and friends and to generations.

Be smart to save, when you work
hard to make money, you must
be wise to work to keep your
wealth.

Affirmations: I am a pride to my family and the
world, I know how to manage resources. I am
a perfect example.

Whoso curseth his

father or his mother, his lamp shall be put

out in obscure

darkness.

Pro 20:20

Never ever curse your parents or the

parents of others

even jokingly.

Affirmations: I am responsible and

reasonable, I am fun but still respectful to

others online or offline.

He that gathereth in summer is a wise

son: but he that sleepeth in harvest

is a son that causeth shame.

Pro 10:5

In the lips of him that hath understanding wisdom is found: but a rod is for the back of him that is void of understanding.

Pro 10:13

You are judged by the things
you do or do not do.
Affirmations: I am a child but I have good
judgment of situations of the physical and
spiritual world around me. I am pure, I am
light.

Even a child is known by his doings, whether his work be pure, and whether it be right.

Pro 20:11

It's either Wisdom or foolishness that is
heard from whatever you say and life
punishes you for not being wise.
Find out wisdom for yourself and you will
save yourself from a lot of beating,
physically, spiritually and emotionally.
Affirmations: I am blessed because I found the
wise ways to do things, I am amazing.

Pride is when you feel too big.

Pride prevents you from

achieving good things for your

self and others.

Avoid pride.

Pride is a limiting factor.

Affirmations: I put pride and ego under

control and I achieve success without shame or

excuses.

When pride cometh, then cometh

shame

Pro 11:2

Integrity is wisdom.
You, your children and your
generations after you, will be blessed
because of integrity.

Affirmations: I am a child of a blessed man and
a man of integrity and my children are blessed
because of me.

The just man walketh in

his integrity: his children are blessed after

him.

Pro 20:7

The righteous is more
excellent than his neighbour:
but the way of the wicked
seduceth them.

Pro 12:26

You bring a curse on yourself when you
treat your parents wrong by your actions
or by verbal abuse.
Never disgrace your parents. Cover up
their indiscretions when they offend you
or the people you love. Be wise.
Affirmations: I am wise, I respect my parents,
elders and everyone. I am in turn respected not
by force but by love.

He that wasteth his

father, and chaseth away his mother, is

a son that causeth shame, and bringeth

reproach.

Pro 19:26

Remember, you are better than a wicked

person, never get enticed by the

things wicked people do.

Be wise.

Affirmations: I am righteous, I am excellent, I

am a leader in good. I choose wisdom.

Na only mumu no dey take advice.

Use your tongue count your teeth.

Only the unwise do not take advice or instructions that can help him/her. Affirmations: I am wise, I learn from the instructions and experiences of older or other people. I grateful, I excel daily.

Chasten thy son while there is hope,
and let not thy soul spare for his
crying.

Pro 19:18

A STITCH IN TIME SAVES NINE.

No person is too young or old for correction.

Make that correction today.

Affirmations: I retrace my steps with wisdom, I understand the measures my parents put in place to help me live my best possible life, I don't see them as punishment but as stepping stones or the elevator to the best me.

A wise son heareth his

father's instruction:

but a scorner heareth not rebuke.

Pro 13:1

He that spareth his rod hateth his son:

but he that loveth him chasteneth

him betimes.

Pro 13:24

Do not ever make your parents,

especially you father think or feel that

your birth into his family was a disaster

or bad luck.

Affirmations: I am divinely guided to bring joy

and peace into my family.

*A foolish son is the
calamity of his father: and the contentions
of a wife are a continual
dropping.*

Pro 19:13

If you don't want to be severely
punished by your parents, try
to do the right things.
Ask God for help if you are
struggling to know the right
things to do.

Affirmations: I happily receive instructions for
living from God and my parents and I'm
glad I do right always.

If you have the fear and respect for
God, you have wisdom and you are
guaranteed a life of assurance and safety.
Affirmations: I and my generation is protected
because I obey the laws of nature which are the
laws of God. I and my family are blessed

A foolish son is a grief to his father, and

bitterness to her that bare him

Pro 17:25

Run away from stupid behaviours so that

you can be happy.

When your parents are happy with you,

you will definitely be happy too.

Affirmations: I am the pride of my mother and

the joy of my father and my relatives because I

am wise and successful.

In the fear of the LORD is strong

confidence: and his children shall have

a place of refuge

Pro 14:26

A fool despiseth his father's

instruction: but he that regardeth

reproof is prudent.

Pro 15:5

Always Remember that you are

not a curse but a blessing to your parents

and you were born to bring joy to

their lives. Do not destroy the joy of you

being their child by your foolish actions

and decisions. Wise up.

Affirmations: I make myself, my parents, my

family, my community and my generation happy

and proud to have me.

He that begetteth a fool doeth it to his

sorrow: and the father of a fool hath

no joy.

Pro 17:21

Stupidity makes you feel like you are
wiser than your parents and older
people.
Specialized education doesn't make
you wiser in handling life's
dynamic issues.
Listen and take instructions.
Affirmations: I am wise to obey my parents in
the way of God.

Don't be too stubborn.

Dem say over stubbornness dey kill.

Try to obey so that you can live.

Affirmations: I am alive, I am grateful to have

people who care about me and are willing to show

me the way of life.

Children's children are the crown of old men; and the glory of children are their fathers.

Pro 17:6

YOU ARE YOUR PARENTS
BEST POSESSION.

Affirmations: I am aware of the love of
my parents and family, I am grateful.

Correction is grievous unto him that forsaketh the way: and he that hateth reproof shall die.

Pro 15:10

A wise son maketh a glad father: but a

foolish man despiseth his mother.

Pro 15:20

Being born with a silver spoon doesn't

guarantee you your crown.

You must be wise not to loose

your inheritance to your servant.

Affirmations: I am co hair with Christ, I am

honourable and a leader, I am wise in all my

ways. I make my siblings and family

proud.

A wise servant shall have rule over a son that causeth shame, and shall have part of the inheritance among the brethren.

Pro 17:2

No matter who or what your

parents are, rich, poor, good, bad,

beautiful, ugly, healthy, sick, wicked or kind, one of your
primary goals must be to bring joy to their lives and make them

proud of who you are because you are

not a curse but a blessing.

Affirmations: I am a wise child, I am a blessing

to my parents and family.

When you do wrong and you take
correction and do not repeat your
mistakes, you are wise.
Affirmations: I am divinity, I am intelligent, my
conscious and subconscious self chooses what is
right for me every time.

He that refuseth

instruction despiseth his own soul: but

he that heareth reproof

getteth understanding.

Pro 15:32

Life is beautiful like I always say and sure life could be truly beautiful with the right amount of cash available to you. Being able to afford things without the fear of going broke is of utmost importance for everybody or almost everybody I know. Due of the quest of staying afloat most people have found themselves in the most hardship one could possibly imagine.

People have different reasons for wanting to be rich, which to me is their personal business, no one should be chastised or bullied for wanting to be rich or have luxuries as they deem fit.

The question is, in your quest for getting what you want, is it fair to all concerned? Would it be okay if some other person

Does the same thing you intend to do to others to get that thing you want? This is why the bible has made it easy and clear for you that you can be wealthy and still be righteous in the eyes of Higher powers and other humans who we are privileged to occupy this earth together at this point in time.

We should therefore always remember that as the sky is wide enough to accommodate all birds without them hurting each other so also the resources available in the world is more than enough to accommodate all of our individual demands and claims at wealth or material riches so there is absolutely no need to perpetrate evil against another just to be rich.

The most important thing you need is to use your brain, think of what you really want. There are fundamentally different,

Diverse and too many ways to make wealth. Which ever way you choose, you must include the use of your intellect, i.e mental work and action which in other words is physical work.

You have to choose which type of work you will place above the other, physical or mental exertion. Mental/intellectual work has to do with creativity like writing, talking, music etc while physical work has to do with physical activities like construction sales, medical practice etc.

Which of the two are you ready to exchange for money? One could also combine both the mental and physical to make money, and the more money you make amount to the wealth or riches you have.

Accumulating wealth through Physical work depends mostly on the amount of time you are willing to give in exchange for money while accumulating wealth by mental or creative work depends largely on the quality of you work and your marketing/distribution strategy.

One thing should be clear that no matter what you are offering in exchange for money, there is always a market or someone willing to exchange money for it.Age, ethnicity or educational back- ground has nothing to do in accumulating wealth.

Having clarified some fundamental truths about getting paid, or making money I want you to take an ex-ray of your life, your thoughts and beliefs.What are you thinking about most of the time? Enough money or not enough money? Scarce resources or abundant resources? What do you believe?

Take a critical look around you, they say there is not enough water, really? But the earth is made up of ¼.% of water! They say people are dying of hunger, not enough food, very funny! Fruits and veggies are getting spoilt and eateries throw food away and they still make profits. Do I have to remind you that Fruits and veggies also grow wild on their own, provided by nature for man- kind and animals. Do not fall into the propaganda being perpetuated against nature by corny business people brainwashing you to think of scarcity.

Life can truly be beautiful if we recognize that all we need is already provided for. We only need to exchange something to Get what we want.

So many bible passages especially in this book of proverbs written by the richest man of bible times clearly says you can't be idle, you must give to receive and everyone has something to give. Chose or decide what you want to give in exchange for that money you so want. When you get your money, know that Money also is a means of exchange for other things you want.

My brief explanations or thoughts about the verses is to give you an insight or broaden your mind concerning the verse, those are my thoughts, as I read through the book of proverbs, I discovered that wisdom is truly the principal thing. The bible seem too complicated to read or has too much information, this is my attempt to simplify and group together verses from the book of wisdom concerning the bible's instructions and admonitions on wealth and riches.

Affirmations help you control your thoughts and keep you focused on what you really want to achieve. Affirmations will help control external forces and how you relate, take in or discard things opposing views to universal truths.

As you read, you can formulate your own affirmation as the situation arises, this helps you get in touch with your higher self, the GOD in you and your subconscious mind will help you take the right decisions and steps and you will find yourself doing the right without fear. Fear they say is an illusion, it's not real.

Conquer your fears with affirmations and find yourself living the Life Of your luxurious and wealthy dreams in this life time.

The sky is your starting point, wealth and riches and happiness are your birthright. Live free! Live wealthy! God speed.